DISCOVERING THE UNITED STATES

Maryland

BY ANGELA LIM

Kids Core
An Imprint of Abdo Publishing
abdobooks.com

abdobooks.com

Published by Abdo Publishing, a division of ABDO, PO Box 398166, Minneapolis, Minnesota 55439.

Printed in China.
052024
092024

Cover Photo: Sean Pavone/Shutterstock Images
Interior Photos: Bettmann/Getty Images, 4–5; Christopher Mazmanian/Shutterstock Images, 6, 29 (bottom left); Brian A. Wolf/Shutterstock Images, 9 (top left); Shutterstock Images, 9 (top right), 9 (bottom left); Radomir Rezny/Shutterstock Images, 9 (bottom right); Jon Bilous/Shutterstock Images, 10; Jeff Taylor/The Winchester Star/AP Images, 12–13; Filip Bjorkman/Shutterstock Images, 15; Eric Espada/Getty Images Sports/Getty Images, 16; Christian Hinkle/Shutterstock Images, 18; Kevin Ruck/Shutterstock Images, 20–21, 29 (bottom right); Wendy Farrington/Shutterstock Images, 23; Kenneth Keifer/Shutterstock Images, 24; Sergey Novikov/Shutterstock Images, 26; Red Line Editorial, 28 (top), 29 (top); Eliyahu Yosef Parypa/Shutterstock Images, 28 (bottom)

Editor: Haley Williams
Series Designer: Katharine Hale

Library of Congress Control Number: 2023949348

Publisher's Cataloging-in-Publication Data

Names: Lim, Angela, author.
Title: Maryland / by Angela Lim
Description: Minneapolis, Minnesota: Abdo Publishing, 2025 | Series: Discovering the United States | Includes online resources and index.
Identifiers: ISBN 9781098293901 (lib. bdg.) | ISBN 9798384913177 (ebook)
Subjects: LCSH: U.S. states--Juvenile literature. | Maryland--History--Juvenile literature. | Northeastern States--Juvenile literature. | Physical geography--United States--Juvenile literature.
Classification: DDC 973--dc23

All population data taken from:
"Estimates of Population by Sex, Race, and Hispanic Origin: April 1, 2020 to July 1, 2022." *US Census Bureau, Population Division*, June 2023, census.gov.

CONTENTS

Artists have drawn Francis Scott Key, *center*, watching the battle over Fort McHenry.

CHAPTER 1

"The Star-Spangled Banner"

It was September 13, 1814. Cannon fire rang out through the night at Fort McHenry in Baltimore, Maryland. British forces swarmed the fort. The United States had been at war with Great Britain for two years. They were fighting over blocked trading routes.

Today, people can visit the historic Fort McHenry in Baltimore, Maryland.

Fort McHenry overlooked the Baltimore **harbor**. American lawyer Francis Scott Key was on a ship in the harbor. He watched as British ships fired rockets at the fort. Cannonballs struck nearby ships. Smoke filled the air. Fighting continued through the night.

In the morning, Key was not sure who had won the battle. The British could have taken over Fort McHenry. That would mean the British would be in control of Baltimore. Key watched as a flag was raised over Fort McHenry. The US flag waved in the wind. American forces had won.

Key felt inspired by the victory. He began to write a poem titled "The Star-Spangled Banner." It would later become the lyrics to the national anthem of the United States.

Land

Maryland is part of the South region of the United States. Pennsylvania borders Maryland to the north. To the south of the state is Virginia.

West Virginia is to the west. And Delaware and the Atlantic Ocean form the eastern border.

The Chesapeake Bay extends into Maryland from Virginia. This body of water connects to the Atlantic Ocean. The Chesapeake Bay runs for about 195 miles (315 km). It is located in the eastern part of the state. Maryland also has **plains** and mountains.

Regions of Maryland

Maryland can be divided into three regions. The easternmost region includes coastal plains. This area has a low **elevation**. The Piedmont region is in central Maryland. It has rolling hills. The Appalachian region is in the western part of the state. Elevation is highest there.

Maryland Facts

DATE OF STATEHOOD
April 28, 1788

CAPITAL
Annapolis

POPULATION
6,164,660

AREA
12,406 square miles
(32,131 sq km)

STATE BIRD

Baltimore oriole

STATE TREE

White oak

STATE FLOWER

Black-eyed Susan

STATE DOG

Chesapeake Bay retriever

Each US state has a different population, size, and capital city. States also have state symbols.

Climate

Maryland has mild temperatures year-round.

Rain is common in the state throughout the year.

Winters in Maryland are usually mild. Temperatures average about 30 degrees Fahrenheit (−1°C).

But snowfall is uncommon. Western Maryland is more likely to have snow than eastern Maryland.

The state gets some types of extreme weather. Hurricanes and tropical storms often occur in August and September. These natural disasters cause flooding and power outages. Tornadoes and wildfires also affect the state.

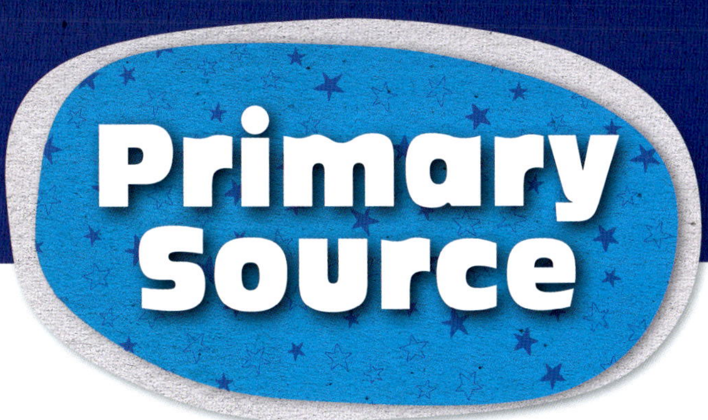

The first part of Francis Scott Key's poem "The Star-Spangled Banner" includes these lines:

> And the rocket's red glare, the bombs
> bursting in air,
> Gave proof through the night that our flag
> was still there . . .

Source: "The Lyrics." *Smithsonian*, n.d., amhistory.si.edu. Accessed 2 Oct. 2023.

Comparing Texts

Think about the quote. How does it connect to the information in this chapter? Or does it give a different perspective? Explain how in a few sentences.

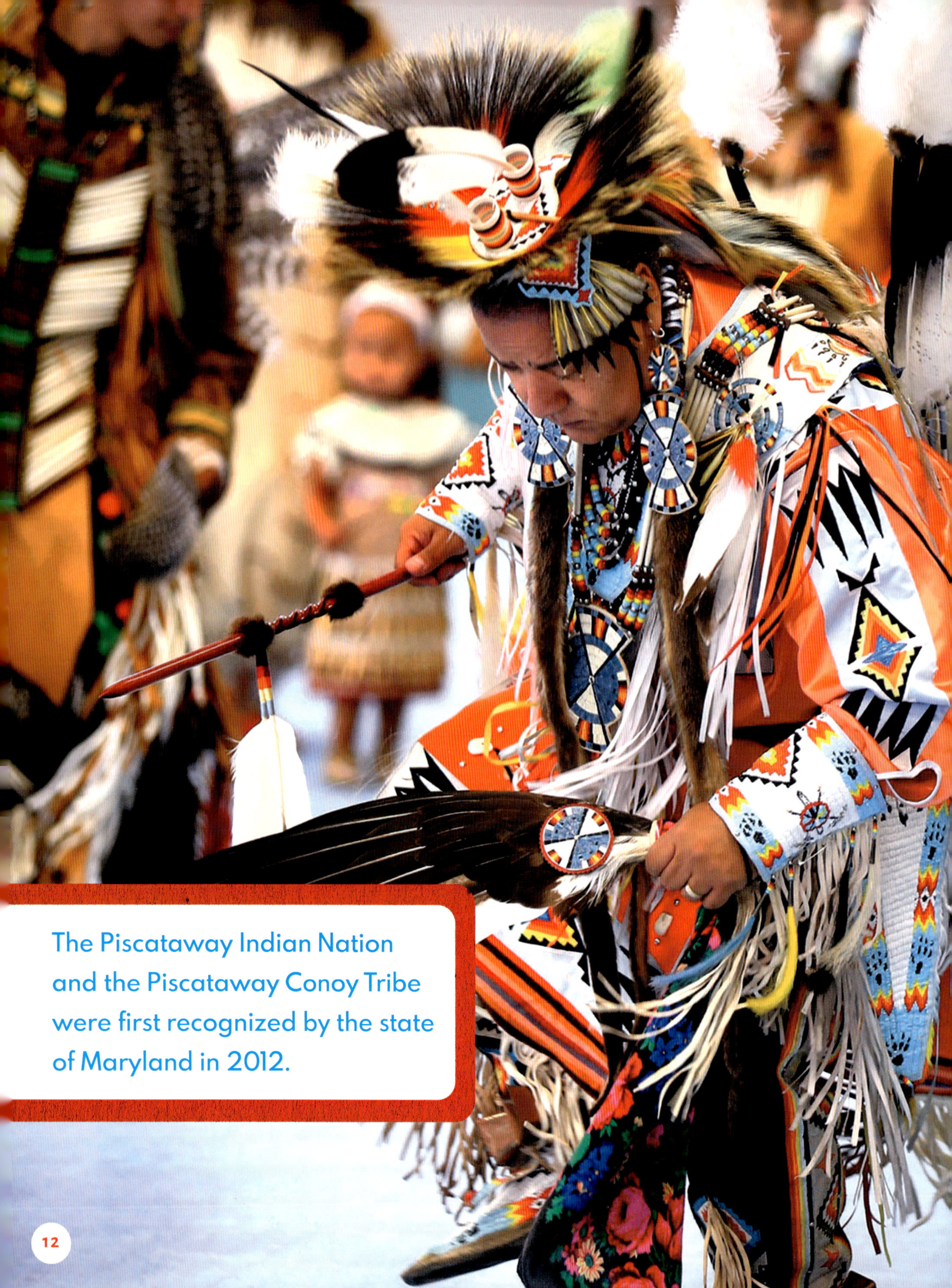

The Piscataway Indian Nation and the Piscataway Conoy Tribe were first recognized by the state of Maryland in 2012.

CHAPTER 2

The People of Maryland

The first people arrived in what is now Maryland about 10,000 years ago. Approximately 8,000 American Indians lived in the region by 1000 BCE. They belonged to 40 different nations. Many of these nations spoke Algonquian languages.

Today, Maryland has no federally recognized tribes. But the state recognizes three tribes. They are the Piscataway Indian Nation, the Piscataway Conoy Tribe, and the Accohannock Indian Tribe.

European **colonists** first came to the Maryland region in 1634. They began to take over the land. Many American Indians were forced to leave their homes.

The colonists brought enslaved African people with them. Slavery became legal in Maryland in 1664. It remained legal until 1864. In 1865, the US government passed a law that made slavery illegal throughout the country.

In 2022, more than 6.1 million people lived in Maryland. About 48 percent of the people

Maryland is the only US state that has a flag based on when it was ruled by Great Britain. The flag's patterns represent two important families in Maryland's early history.

were white. More than 31 percent were Black. Hispanic and Latino people made up 11 percent of the population. And about 7 percent of people were Asian.

Baltimore Ravens fans often wear the team's purple and black colors on game days.

Culture

Food and sports are key parts of Maryland's culture. Seafood such as crab cakes are famous in Maryland. Old Bay seasoning is often sprinkled on top of seafood dishes. The seasoning contains spices including bay leaf, mustard, and paprika.

Baltimore is home to a few major professional sports teams. The Baltimore Ravens are part of the National Football League (NFL). Baseball fans can watch the Orioles play in Camden Yards. Swimmer Michael Phelps is from Baltimore. He won 23 Olympic gold medals.

Maryland Arts Scene

Maryland has a big arts scene. People can watch plays and musicals at the Cumberland Theater in western Maryland. The Maryland Symphony Orchestra performs in Hagerstown. There are also many art **galleries** throughout the state.

Some coastal cities in Maryland have large marinas. Fishers keep their boats here.

Industry

Maryland has several major industries. The state borders Washington, DC. Because of this, many government employees work in Maryland. Some work for the US military. They may help develop and produce weapons. Others protect top secret information.

Fishing is another top industry in Maryland. The state produces the most blue crabs of any

US state. Striped bass and oysters are also part of the state's fishing industry. The Chesapeake Bay is a major fishing spot.

Many scientists have jobs in Maryland. Some work at major universities. This includes Johns Hopkins University in Baltimore. Others work at places run by the US government. These scientists may develop **vaccines** that help prevent people from getting sick.

Explore Online

Visit the website below. Does it give any new information about Maryland that wasn't in Chapter Two?

Maryland

abdocorelibrary.com/discovering-maryland

Baltimore's Inner Harbor reminds people about how the city has changed over time.

CHAPTER 3

Places in Maryland

Baltimore is the most **populated** city in Maryland. It is located in north-central Maryland. Baltimore lies just west of the Chesapeake Bay. Visitors to the city can stroll along the Inner Harbor. The harbor has restaurants and shops.

It also has attractions such as the Maryland Aquarium and the Maryland Science Center.

Frederick is another large Maryland city. It is in western Maryland. People can enjoy views of the Allegheny Mountains there. They can also go hiking and explore the outdoors.

Ocean City is a popular vacation spot. It sits on the shores of the Atlantic Ocean. Visitors can swim, surf, and kayak in the water.

Seashores and State Parks

There is plenty to do outside Maryland's cities. Assateague Island is in the Atlantic Ocean. The majority of the island belongs to Maryland. The rest belongs to Virginia. Assateague Island

The horses on Assateague Island have split into small groups that live and travel together.

is a national seashore. Wild horses roam the beaches. People can enjoy outdoor activities such as camping and fishing on the island.

Muddy Creek Falls is about 54 feet (16 m) tall.

Swallow Falls State Park is in western Maryland. The park has several waterfalls. Muddy Creek Falls is the most famous. People can enjoy hikes with stunning mountain views in the park. They can also go white water rafting on the Youghiogheny River.

Sandy Point State Park is on the western shore of the Chesapeake Bay. People can enjoy scenic views of the bay while picnicking. They can also go boating.

Landmarks

Maryland has many historic landmarks. Fort McHenry is where Francis Scott Key wrote the words to the national anthem. The fort was also used during the American Civil War (1861–1865). Today, people can watch how the fort's cannons were once used.

Antietam

Many Civil War battles took place in Maryland, such as the deadly Battle of Antietam. More than 22,000 soldiers were killed or wounded during this battle. The Antietam National Cemetery honors the fallen soldiers.

The Maryland State House was built between 1772 and 1779.

The Maryland State House is another important landmark. The capitol building is in Annapolis. It is the oldest state capitol building still in use in the United States.

Maryland attracts many types of visitors. People come to the state to learn about US history. They enjoy beautiful views of mountains and beaches. They may cheer on sports teams in Baltimore. Or they can try seafood by the Chesapeake Bay. There are many things to see and do in Maryland.

Further Evidence

Look at the website below. Does it give any new evidence to support Chapter Three?

Chesapeake Bay

abdocorelibrary.com/discovering-maryland

State Map

KEY

Capital

Park

City or town

Point of interest

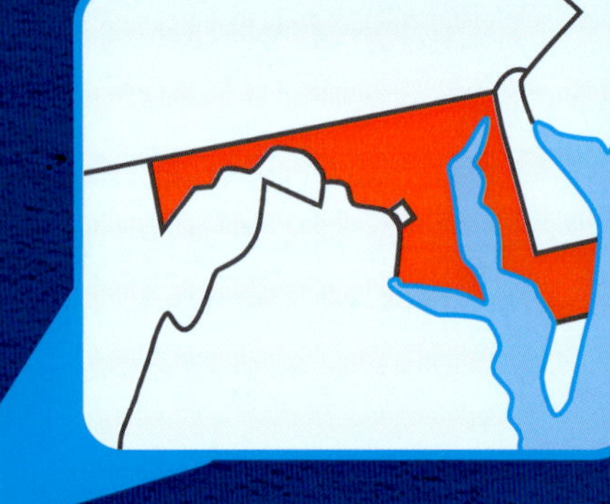

Maryland: The Free State

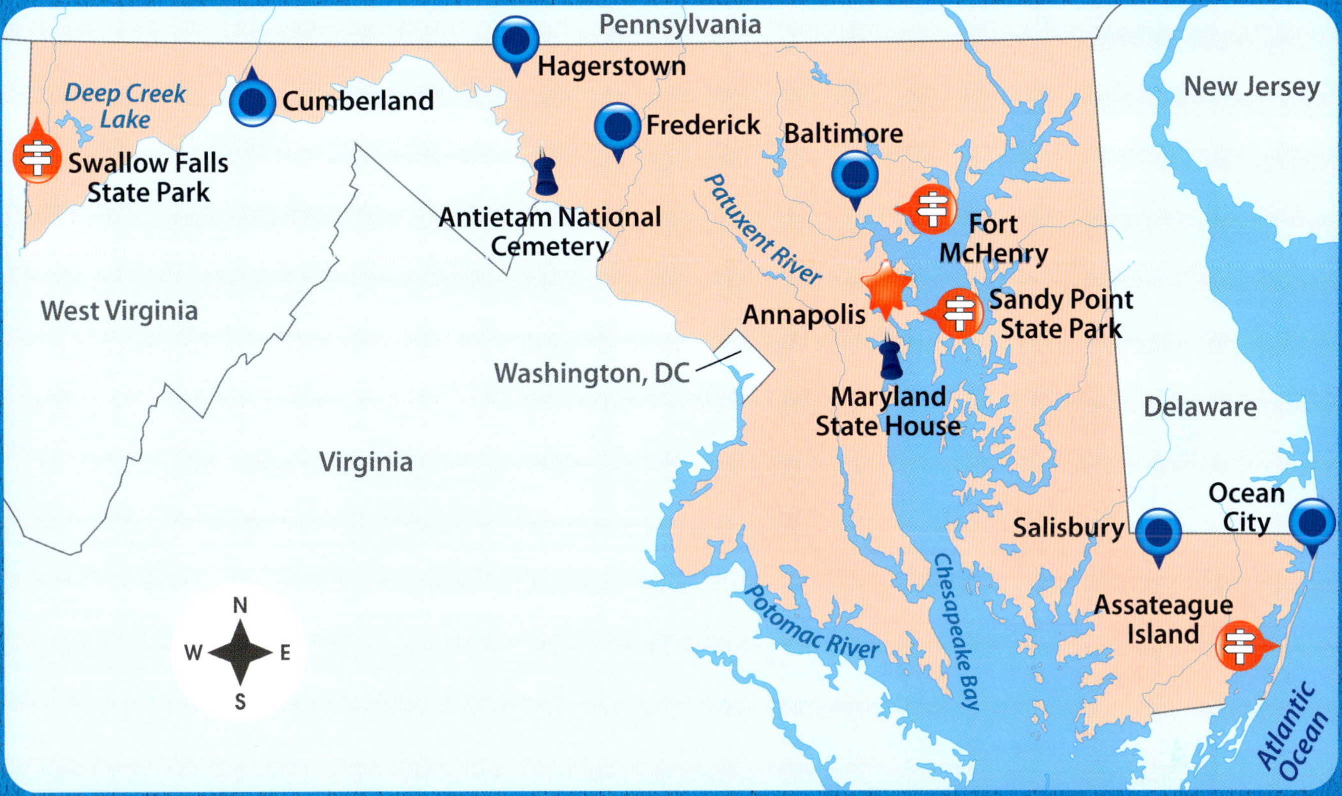

Pennsylvania
Hagerstown
Deep Creek Lake
Cumberland
Swallow Falls State Park
Frederick
Baltimore
Antietam National Cemetery
Patuxent River
Fort McHenry
New Jersey
West Virginia
Annapolis
Sandy Point State Park
Washington, DC
Maryland State House
Delaware
Virginia
Ocean City
Salisbury
Assateague Island
Potomac River
Chesapeake Bay
Atlantic Ocean
N
W
E
S

Fort McHenry

Baltimore

Glossary

colonists
people who have moved to and taken control of an area

elevation
the height above sea level

galleries
rooms or buildings where art is displayed

harbor
an area of deep water near the shore where ships can dock

plains
areas of flat, treeless land

populated
settled or lived in

vaccines
medicines that are given to help protect people from diseases

Online Resources

To learn more about Maryland, visit our free resource websites below.

Visit **abdocorelibrary.com** or scan this QR code for free Common Core resources for teachers and students, including vetted activities, multimedia, and booklinks, for deeper subject comprehension.

Visit **abdobooklinks.com** or scan this QR code for free additional online weblinks for further learning. These links are routinely monitored and updated to provide the most current information available.

Learn More

Berne, Emma Carlson. *The History of the American Revolution*. Rockridge, 2021.

Meier, William. *Baltimore Ravens*. Abdo, 2020.

Murray, Julie. *Maryland*. Abdo, 2020.

Index

About the Author

Angela Lim is an MFA student in poetry at Indiana University in Bloomington, Indiana.